In My Feelings

James McQueen

In My Feelings Copyright © 2014

Sunny Smiles Company

ALL RIGHTS RESERVED

ISBN: 9780692256930

CONTENTS

Dedication 1
Issues of Life 7
Peace of Life 30
Love of Life 45
Religion of Life 75
About The Author 88

INSPIRATIONAL DEDICATION

I wish you were here not to fill you with my problems with my pain; but to make you proud. For what I've made of your name! I see that life can be misunderstood, confusing and a challenge. So me looking up to you as a man and now I am a man I have a true life understanding. No regrets no complaints just me, my life, and kids with you in our everyday planning! Until I see you in heaven I might just drop a tear. I got you across my chest that's how bad I wish you were here.

2 my OG James McQueen A.K.A Cokey

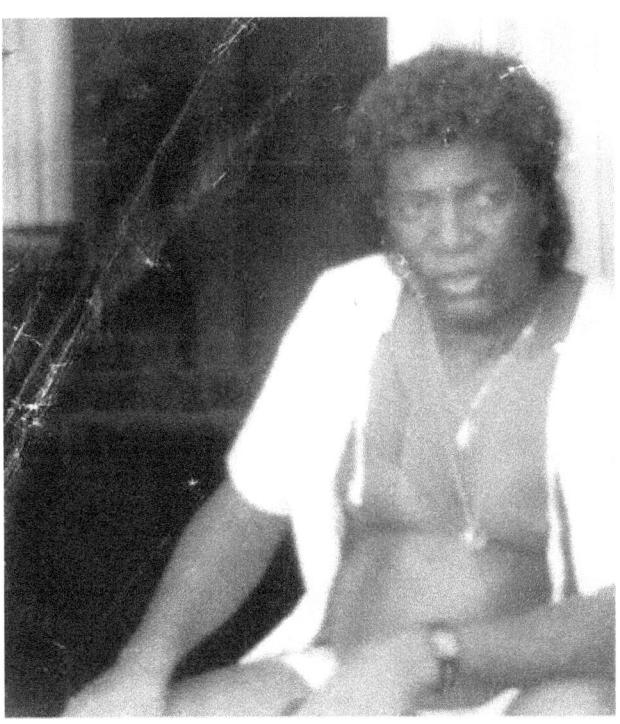

DEDICATION

Thank you first and for most to my Lord and Savior Jesus Christ; followed by that person who is and will always been in my heart. The rest goes to the Mad Hatta show and 97.9 the box for providing laughter thru pain. Rich Homie Quan for making me understand that ignorance guided by intelligence is a true art form; as for everybody and anything else.

Thank you for the inspiration.

ISSUES OF LIFE

ASSPIRATIONS OF LOVE

Have you ever been in a room of pretend?
While you hoping for love to begin
The strain between faith and hope
Until you just can't cope.
The room is full of blood line that's life time. Familiar?
Praying the hurt won't kill ya
But shit you grow numb in the end!
Because you neva knew it actually was a room of pretend!

BE TRUE TO YOU

Real is Real. How to be a grown up?
That's just like asking what's my purpose in life?
Well here it is. I don't know everything.
This I do know;
you can't halfway do neither one.
So live life to the fullest
and if you need directions
confide in Jesus.
And being grown,
if you halfway doing that,
really means you not ready
You just wanna be grown.
You just want a title of.
Quit bullshitting you!

CHANCE

There's a good chance it won't hurt no more.
There's a good chance time will be well spent again!
There's a good chance that my heart will beat again wit joy and not pain! There's a good chance that there's a good chance!

CONFIDENCE

Why errbody did sumthin to you? But whats strange is the people involved is just them. Now for errbody to do sumthin to you! You have to be involved . So stop wit the nonsense and bring truth to the light . You do it to you and errbody just bein them. Either way you be alright wit you and stop giving errbody a chance to do sumthin to you.
@Sarcasm kills!

DAMN FOOL

Have you ever kicked it wit somebody
you knew you wasn't but did it
anyway and found out why
and that's the reason you shouldn't have?
Have you ever did sumthin wit somebody
you knew you wasn't
but did it anyway?
And then wonder why?
Well there's your answer.
Cuz you knew even after a time or two
and u chose to
send you through hell
and you wasn't even supposed to
fuck wit her or him.
Damn fool!

DAMN YOU

Pride I can't stand you
dude you hurt every possibility in my life.
Like I really love my lady but I listen to you and
don't show it
Like for example I need a job
coulda had a job but you said its fast food
and now I'm actually introducing my kids to you,
hell naw, damn you pride.
I'm gone leave and not look back,
but is that just my PRIDE talkin?

DESTINY

I really don't like sharin you
Even when I wasn't havin you
Though it may seem crazy.
But why else would I still be loving you and not wit you?
And as our paths lead us so far away .
How tha hell I wind up back with you to this day?
God made you for me and me for you.
I really don't like sharin you.

FIGHT NIGHT

Did I do that
or did you
cuz I can't tell
through all the hell
we been through.
On just sum dry to tell another lie
See tears fall from each other's eyes.
And then we have the nerves, fuck, make up, fall in love
again without processin what we did.
Hopefully wishing on make it last forever.
So again im askin did I do that or you?
Cause I can't tell all the hell we been through.

FLIP SIDE

It's amazing what we established as kids,
and as adults we fuck up!
Like for instance
we forsaken all others and didn't even know what that
was as kids.
We fought for each other as kids.
Had no agenda as kids.
We both knew without even knowingly trying to but ended
up heart over heels for each other as kids.
As adults we added shit,
talk shit ,
fight hard as shit,
fuck up shit ,
manipulate shit!
And act like we don't remember shit.
Or how we were as KIDS!
@GO Fuck yo self!

I'M GOOD

I be fucked up and still good
Financially I'm fucked up
Spiritually I'm good,
Fucked up relationship wise
but she aint the last and fa damn sho wasn't the first.
So mentally I'm good.
I'm fucked up with family but fam is fam.
You can't change DNA.
So physically I'm good but here's tha catch.
Through all that fuckery I clearly understood.
My Jesus walked with me through it all
And showed me that I'm good.

KARMA

If all of your tomorrows have caught up to you right now,
and it looks like yesterday
you clearly did something wrong
or took a wrong turn.
Focus on right now,
leave yesterday were it is at
and make sure
when tomorrow gets here that it looks better from what you
did
with right now!

MID-LIFE RIGHTEOUS

I woke up wit dick problems! I had baby moist and wet ,
Ready to crash and burn like an air force vet!
But when it came to lift off I stayed on tha ground .
So between my hand and my tongue I had to cool
baby engine down and tha pussy gladiator in me got my
brain goin for a round.
Is this it?
Has the day come were old dude has become a old dude!
Am I finna have to embrace viagra to solve em?
Shit fuck that!
I'm 39 but my dick 19
and I jus woke up wit dick problems!

NEAR SIGHTED

What's so hard about the truth?
Is it that really hard to own up?
But quick to say I'm supposed to trust!
But what's sad is you lie to yourself so you believe the lies you tell me.
And my love is supposed to stay the same while you pretend that it's not a game.
But at all ends where the truth is missin there's a lie!
So again I ask
What's so hard about the truth?

OUCH

I was scared and you didn't understand.
I yelled and you got mad.
I was hurt and from what I could see that was a good thing.
There's always feelings on both sides but you hurt now.
So when I was scared and hurt what was the difference?
Oh I know. Yours hurt more than mine?
Ouch!

PAY ATTENTION

Why sleep and settle for what they offering.
Why kill time when time well spent is far better headed to the coffin.
Why be clueless when that rhymes with useless.
If you don't get it by now then you never will!
Born to be great!

REASON FOR THE SEASON

Tis tha season:
for what though?
Your selfish intentions or tha love that flows freely
I might add freely twice cuz selfish is ugly!
I just want for tha season to be what it is for love, cheer,
and unconditional giving with no agenda. Just love no pretenda !
Amen

REVELATION

It all make since now!
I been make n progress wit out process!
I been try n 2 create better an not kno n what better is!
An really got errbody str8 except 4 self!
So who did what 2 who?
Shit I did it 2 myself!
It all makes since now!

SICK AND TIRED

Fuck me
naw
fuck you
and this tha last time
I say that shit
you more than what I wanted to chew and for damn sure
way too much to digest!
So while we go in
and clear our chest!
fuck me
naw
fuck you
and this tha last time I say that shit!

SMART ASS DUMMY

Quit tryna make since out of bullshit!
Quit tryna function in dysfunction!
Quit tryna make insanity into brilliance!
Just know I know that I'm not meant to be torn or damaged.
So quit tryna!

STATISTIC

Man.
Long summers,
cool fall, thermal wear in winters,
Spring break
in spring.
Turned into
hustle summer, locked up fall, out on bond winter,
See you three springs later.
From a black child
to a black
statistic!

UNDERSTANDING YOU

And it begins:
When is right, right?
When you want it to b right or how it should've been right?
Or how it could've been right?
Or how you compromise facts to make right, right?
How about this?
Let's just let right be right in the sense it was
mean't to be ALRIGHT?

WHAT WORLD

What world you living in
where you feel like
you can just wake up
and go get everything ever body else has
without a job?
What world you living in
where you feel like
you can go take from people
who work hard?
What world you living in
to get yo self locked up
with no regard?
I really don't understand.
What world you really living in?

PEACE OF LIFE

HIGH STATE OF MIND

I just wanna be cool
Get fucked up and do what cool fucked up people do
Maybe dance till we both get horny.
Or maybe we fuck till we both get tha munchies.
Or be cool and do our best song impersonations.
And laugh at each other
Look in each other eyes and visualize about being together.
I really don't give a fuck what we do.
Long as its along tha lines of bein cool!
I just wanna be cool.

GHETTO FAME

Street light raised. Concrete paid.
For errytime I was under a street light.
I gotta admit I felt like I was on stage and my act
was number one dope dealer.
I caught concrete errytime.
I had to pay for gettin away with bein on stage
but I can say I never been the one to make some
other pay for my already paid dues no snitchin
allowed.
But between my acts and my payments its a
beautiful thing cuz it feels good to know who you are and
really be him. Stay cool and keep it 1000!

PLEASE AND THANK YOU

Please and thank you.
If I wasn't what you thought;
well I live up to my own expectation.
Please and thank you.
I never meant to scar or damage.
Cuz I'm better than your average.
Please and thank you.
But if there is any doubt.
About anything pertaining to this black intelligent male
That you might not feel is accountable or true.
Well you can just not be bothered.
Please and thank you.

SHINE

I shine without tryin.
You fucked up on what you wear.
How you buy it.
How long you and yo life experience gone stay on stage
Being temporary minded?
Be genuine and official with yo damn self.
Stop all that damn fakin, frontin, and lyin.
It really feels good wit nothing to prove.
Cuz I shine wit out tryin!!!

SAILING BEYOND

I'm smiling while I'm cussin .
You all caught up with tha hollerin and fussin!
Shit you don't see my point and I don't see yours
which leaves us with nothing.
And yes feelins are flowin
so things are kind of touchin!
But all tha while its not that serious.
Cuz im still smiling while I'm cussin!
Blah blah blah blah.

FAMILY

Nowadays that's how family is.
I used to be part of your every day
But that seems so long ago and so far away.
Is it just me or do I really want to know where we stop bein fam?
And now that we grown we barely speak.
Instead of the company we used to keep.
So for now I'm gone enjoy
U, Yu, and You
in the moment and take it for what it is.
Because nowadays that's how family is.

INTRODUCTION

What's good?
That's what's up.
What's ham?
What up god?
What it C like?
What it B like?
Oh boi!
Ya bish.
Can ya dig it?
What's tha science?
Whoadie.
Word homie.
Holla back.
How about
CAN I GET A SIMPLE HELLO?

REALLY

Man how did I do that?
I don't know!
When did I do that?
Shit I guess so!
Are you sure that's the way it go?
If not its done so you got to let it GO!
Oh Well!

SETTLING

We good till we ain't just good no mo!
We hood till we take time to grow.
We should but sometimes we don't even know.
We love even when we don't know how it go.
So we good till we ain't just good no mo.

THANKFUL

I been walking this life all alone
and sometimes it gets hard to hold on.
But the road gets easier as I grow old
despite all my gripes an moans.
So what I do now is keep lookin straight ahead.
Stay cool through it all an instead.
I smile cause what's the point if you alive but wanna be
dead?

THINKING

It's amazing
what I think about
when I sit up
and think about it.
Like for example,
I can't go back
and take away the mistakes.
From deep dark secrets
to the first heartbreak.
Or just plain ole confusion
and let it fester into delusion.
But you know a try beats a
failure and never is not an option,
and my switch stay on I can.
So please pardon my arrogance
when I salute me
for being a real
MAN...

TRUTH

Big homie stay up on yo game.
Don't let smoke and artificial stress fuck up yo brain!
You been had you till OG Jesus came.
Maintain, refresh you and smile thru tha pain.
It's always good to remind you how you stand and continue
to not complain.
Because I step forward take charge, use my faith,
and always maintain.
Bink Good Game

TURN UP

Man my soul feelin good along wit my physical!
I'm just getin dressed but I'm vibin hard wit my spiritual.
Shit I hit the door;
smiles and hands greet me all through the room
Right about that time I hear turn up and I start to consume
my hips of choice ,
my drug of choice,
listenin to my noise of choice,
Turn up!
I woke up butt naked and hungry,
Throw up.
Them damn turn up moments!

WORTH

Girl you ain't worth a booger!
All the unnecessary stress that has been brought about,
all the lies and cries you claim I cause through it all!
Girl you ain't worth a booger!
Swearin I'm the master of deception,
knowin you were the mistress of manipulation!
After all of falling out of yo definition of love as well as
falling out of a whole lot of bullshit just because.
I just had to let you know that!
GIRL YOU AINT WERTH A BOOGER!

LOVE OF LIFE

FOREVER NEVER GOT FOUND

There was a point we said forever.
Now we're on the road of never.
But to make a negative a positive
I look at the growing moments,
the showing moments,
the times we both needed to be held,
the holding moments,
and even though forever was never found.
We will always have them type of moments.
Forever never got found.

A REAL KISS

All you need is a good heart and a good will
to see the sun on a rainy day.
All you need is a real smile and a genuine gesture
to paint the pain away.
At all ends to try and pretend is just hope put on hold.
When the one true virtue is love.
The common goal!

BEIN RICH FOREVER

When will there be a point of clarity between the two of us?
When will we choose humbling self instead of choosing to cuss and fuss?
How bout we make sure we fight for the love instead of fighting over the pain?
That's the only way our love will maintain.
B N Rich 4 Ever.

CAN YOU EXPLAIN

The thing is if you can't control it.
How can you expect to control somebody with it?
While you feelin what you feelin?
I've been high and low in and out and still have not yet to figure it out.
4 you over achieved people wit your accolades.
There's a thing that your accomplished selves can't explain and to truly be successful in it .
You have to ride with it.
Till your whole mind, body, and soul submits to it.
SOMETHING ABOUT LOVE.

COMPREHENSION

This time love I understand.
This time love I'm a man.
This time love I'm not gone try I just am.
This time love if hurt comes about.
I know it didn't come from you.
That wasn't the plan.
This time love I understand.
Life ain't worth life without LOVE!

DAMN KIDS

Kids are truly selfish,
hard headed,
know everything except the right thing.
And I wonder what they would do if I was
not to give a fuck!
Where would they be?
That ain't gone happen cause I really do love and care bout
all my kids.

EXPERIMENT

Could you please stop usin me as an experiment?
I don't know how to play well with others
when it comes to my heart!
But 2 even out the science project let's make a test tube
baby
and if we fail I'm gone enjoy the try.
So take your experiment kit
and let me make it unless we
experimenting on each other.

EYES WIDE SHUT

Girl I'm not tryna hear that shit,
and fuck what you goin through.
All the while I think it's about me,
when really I'm bein insensitive to your needs.
Girl I ain't tryna hear that shit,
and fuck what you goin through.
You comin at me combative
so I do the same to you.
Girl I ain't tryna hear that shit,
And fuck what you goin through.
By now you have hit the door
left me hear in my feelings ,
and thoughts to see what's really true.
So now I pick up the cell take a deep breathe:
Hey where you at? Hey where you at?
Oh you wit that dude?
Well look I apologize, don't move a muscle, I'm on way to you
and I wanna hear errrthang you been goin through.

HAPPY HOME

Let me take my time wit my tongue to change your mind,
about what ever had happened.
Or whoever had did it when they had did it.
My desire is to finesse as well as to make it say meow and
after squirt and leave my chin drippin of curiosity.
Did I do that or did she make it happen?
Either way I got passion while I'm lashin.
I'm gone make you cum to sum kind of conclusion.
No illusions just wet ,warm , and body shakin softly but
uncontrollably!
I had a conversation wit my pet cat.

HATE TO LOVE YOU

How could you hate me for lovin you?
How could you hurt me for scoldin you?
How do you give scars for structure?
How do you give war for peace?
It really amazes me
that a genuine gesture is looked at as pain.
How could you hate me
for loving you?

HOW CAN I

How can I try for love
when love is not there?
How can I hope in loneliness and despair?
How can I be willing to sacrifice me for a simple emotion?
Or is it just me scared of everything that comes with devotion?
Damn how can I?

I CAN ONLY BE ME

I can't think for the both of us.
I can't learn and try to teach the both of us.
If anything I trust I love and that's not good enuff!
I wish sometimes I didn't love the way I love .
Then it wouldn't be heartbreak or an argument
to bring about distrust!
So once again I'm smart and cool
but just for me not for the both of US!
Word

I SALUTE YOU

No matter what we did and how we did
it long as I got to love you.
The easy nights and hard days
long as I got 2 love you.
I remember a time
when it wouldn't have mattered either way, what we do!
but ironic and to me how iconic.
This has been time well spent
keepin on keepin on loving you.

INSTRUCTIONS NEEDED

I understand why Romeo and Juliet killed themselves for
love.
Because unknowingly we actually
fight, cry, lie, and damn near die.
Never really knew what love brings.
It just so happens to happen
and there we go wit no instruction just feelings.
Damn Romeo and Juliet!

JUST WHAT I BEEN MISSING

My first reaction was to push away from you when
I felt my heart jump.
I went along for the ride because I was curious
about this feeling that I felt.
To my surprise it wasn't a whim or a fluke.
It was actually you and I just don't know if this
feeling I'm feeling can still succumb you!
DAMN YOU BEAUTIFUL STRANGER

LOVE

Love wouldn't be love if it was mean't 2 hurt.
Just to know you in expectation of hurt while claiming love.
Did I miss the memo or you just naturally got adjusted to hurt?
To truly know love you got to let love be love.
Anything outside of that is just a distraction.
No rhyme, no jingle, just facts.

LOVE IS FREE

2 take all of me and give 2 you
was 2 easy 1 life I got
and only 1 time
I choose 2 not think and just do.
1 mind and 1 heart 2 never be played wit;
2 never be broke.
2 much love and 1 chance at it.

LOVE AND ITS SIMPLICITY

I give sun,
I get pain,
I give smiles,
I get rain
I give affection,
I get complaints! All this
for tryin
to help you find you! Its all to the good because there's no
agenda
just love
and love
is all we need!

MY TIME

I wonder when the moment of love will truly come my way?
I wonder when sunshine will catch my doorstep and brighten the rest of my days.
I wonder when these weird times we live in will ever get normal?
Until then between love and sin I'm gone be stuck wonderin.

NO OPTION

The same reason I choose not to argue with you .
Is the same reason you choose to argue.
The same reason I choose peace.
Is the same reason you choose war.
I need you to choose to lose forever.
Or choose to find forever.
Either way I'm fine because after all this choosing,
I know I'm gone still love you with all my heart
wit out even choosing to.

RUDE AWAKENING

I remember every word you said when you said enuff is not
enuff and too much is just too much!
I see clearly that my presence as well as my type of help
wasn't for you
I understand that my words that would try to bring about
ease just wasn't .
I can clearly see that the
kool-aid was just a glass of water.
So just know I remember every word you said
when
too much was too much
and
enuff was not enuff.

SON

Say dude I know you chillin right now
and you tryna figure out how.
But while you doin that
I just had to let you know even though
I don't love you the way you want me to
I do, I'm daddy and you son,
we love hard
you gotta get you before I can
and you gotta love you even though I am.
I miss you a whole lotta lotta but before you get free
please love you!
Cause I really do!
No doubt about it!
A father's love.

SPIRITUAL CONNECTION

There's no greater moment than this,
your head on my chest
while my hand on your hip.
Quality time is the idea of love
between two people
where no words can explain just knowin.
Jus being spiritually connecting
and not knowin where it might lead.

STAY FOCUSED ON LOVE

I don't wanna make love bad.
How do you take love and turn it in to hate?
Why not just not be bothered and stay cool?
Thats the problem it feels good and warm
and you want more.
Hurt comes along and hate follows and you
lose hope.
Wait! Remember what it feels like all warm and
good and just breathe and turn hate back into
love.
Don't look back.
Stay focused on LOVE.

SURPRISE

Did you just snatch my heart out my chest and make my stomach weak?
My knees a lil shaky
and I'm sweating on the bottom of my feet.
My hands are clammy from just a look!
Wait a minute shit!
I did just take that blue dolphin.
Damn ecstasy!

THE RECIPE

To try and establish control,
for heartbreak protection
is a bad recipe for a relationship.
You just gotta go with God.
Go with trust and believin love and
ignore the negativity.
Be watchful of what's love's tendencies and what's not.
And if you really really confused just stop.
Because you controlin someone for love
is a bad recipe for a relationship.

BEAUTIFUL

It's so beautiful
even when you don't seem to fulfill the need.
Never the less
proceed to pursue wit no idea of what comes next.
despite of all the storms if your heart stays warm;
you start to trust and on the fact it's beautiful
not looking wit the eye of lust.
Then just know it is so Beautiful!

NUMB

Let me love you till love won't let me; through yo apololies and alibies. Let me love you till love won't let me; through the strain and pain and ill gotten gain. Let me love you till love won't let me; through the storms and screams and broken dreams. Let me love you till love won't let me. I just pray you and me are meant to be.
Jesus let me love till love won't let me.
Amen

LOOK INSIDE

Its 2 cool of a world 2 b frustrated!
But you took this turn and that turn and now you hate it!
But its not tha world's fault!
You chose 2 follow ova bein genuine and chose
lookin cool instead of really bein it!
So rewind. Check you!
Because tha world is just 2 cool 2 b frustrated!

RELIGION OF LIFE

AMEN

Jesus thank you for tha
correction, direction, and protection!
I could not live in this terrible place without:
Your goodness,
Your mercy,
Your grace!

FIGURE ME OUT

Man I be chillin,
Not plotin and schemin
Just chillin
tryna figure me out.
Not usin other people
for an excuse
on why I did what I did
and how I did it .
Shit thats just me.
So until Jesus transforms me into a better me.
Man I'm just gone be chillin.
Tryna figure me out!

FOCUS

Never look back if you missed it.
Never go forward if you don't know where you're going,
and never operate on false pretense
Its just really horrible of you to do.
Stay focused be true to you and you love God.

GOOD AND BAD

The devil's HATE Jesus's LOVE.
That why in those times
you extend your hand in love
you receive hatred back
and you never see it comin.
Count it all joy
because love will find you.

GRACE OF GOD

The only thing I owe you is prayer.
Why is it that I got to invest me into you.
Why is it that I'm worried about you and yo problems
when you continue to do what you do?
I'm tired of thinking my hand as well as my heart helps
you to get through.
When prayer is all I can give as well as owe you.

LOOKING GLASS

Look at reality thru reality eyes.
Don't let trends or society have you wantin more than your life prescribed.
Only Jesus knows if you really need that shake wit them fries.
But until then kill the phasaudes, trends, and imaginative thinking.
Just look at reality through reality EYES!

MY FAITHFUL STANCE

The less I talk and the more I pray,
is the answer to my errday?
The less I talk and the more I pray,
keeps the devil away.
The less I talk the more I pray,
lets Jesus know my dependence is in him
to show me the way!
I got a carnal understanding
which tries to lead me astray.
So I got an on high state of mind ,
which directs me to say
kill all the talk and nonsense.
and continue to pray.

NOT GROWN ENOUGH

How you know betta but won't do betta?
Is it really that hard to take good advice?
Or you jus satisfied making the same mistakes twice?
How you know betta but won't do betta?
Is it that you too damn grown and just don't want to learn?
Or all your lessons have to come wit a scar or a burn?
Just in case you get tired and want some help.
Don't worry I been prayin the whole time.
Just check yo self!
Do betta will come about .
While you picking up your blessings off tha shelf.

REACHING

Im tryna reach in a different way.
I pray to God I'm not bein led astray.
I can big me up but fuck me up at tha same damn time.
I have kept it pushin,
even when failure has defeated my try.
So here goes nothing hope and prayin it turns into
something Because I'm reaching in a different way.

REAL TALK

2 my young 1's; believe in more than money!
You fuckin up you and think tha shit is funny!
Never lookin forward or taking time to think.
Shit get real when that cell go clink!
To my young queens; believe in more than money!
Cause nine times out of ten once you get it,
you turn around and give it to Mr. Dont Give A Fuck.
Or Mr. Getin Them Jeans Fast Honey!
To sell your soul for temporary is just not right.
So understand this message while I type.
Say fuck money and I bet you have more.
Give love and more love will come your way.
Praise Jesus till your dying day!
Now thats something to believe in.
Alright! Alright! Alright!

WHY ASK WHY

Every where all at one time. Stand in one place but touch all different areas wit my mind.
Some times I wonder is this my true design?
I try to talk to Jesus about it .
He tells me to keep trying.
So I guess I'm really mean't to be everywhere all at one time!
Why?

ABOUT THE AUTHOR

James McQueen is an entrepreneur, videographer, husband, and father. Mr. McQueen pursued a life in the street for many years because it was historically and generationally all that he knew. Eventually he decided on a better approach to living to being a positive example for generations to come. Mr. McQueen became an author to inspire his family and others just like he once was to pursue life beyond limitations.